ABOUT
transubstantiations

"All poetry is born of play:" Johan Huizinga writes, "the sacred play of worship, the festive play of courtship, the martial play of contest, the disputatious play of braggadocio, mockery and invective, the nimble play of wit and readiness." Is there a writer or scholar whose work embodies this adage more than Jerome McGann? Whether turning nonsense into new sense in ludic stanzas in the vein of Lear or Nash ("There are rumors / He had had discourse with cats, / Visited vast lunar flats / Watched wasp women's fierce combats," for example, from "Incidents in the Life of my Rebbe Virgil"), traipsing through the cockleburred, visual fields of L=A=N=G=U=A=G=E poetics, or delving with Dickinsonian "Costumeless Consciousness" into the limits of words in confrontation with the ecstatic vicissitudes of love and death, McGann is iconoclastic Romanticist, antic Intellectual, renegade Lyricist—a writer sui generis and very much needed in our moment.

Lisa Russ Spaar

transubstantiations

poetry & verse

Jerome McGann

afterword

Janet Kauffman

Station Hill Press

BARRYTOWN, NY

Published by Station Hill Press, the publishing project of the Institute for Publishing Arts, Inc., 120 Station Hill Road, Barrytown, NY 12507, a not-for-profit, Federally tax-exempt organization [501(c)(3)].

Online catalogue: www.stationhill.org
E-mail: publishers@stationhill.org

Cover art reproduces one of Arthur B. Kennickell's "Untitled" mutimedia works.
Cover and interior design by Susan Quasha.

Library of Congress Catalog Card Number: available
ISBN: 9781581772388

Author's Acknowledgments
Special thanks to George Quasha who called for this book and to Susan Quasha who made it fit for appearing in public. And to the friends who are here and have been talking with these creatures for so many years. And to Virgil Burnett, now "gone into the world of light" that his darkness so deeply comprehended.

Land Acknowledgment
In the spirit of truth and equity, it is with gratitude and humility that we acknowledge that the Institute for Publishing Arts, Inc. and Station Hill Press reside on the sacred homelands of the Munsee and Muhheaconneok people, who are the original stewards of this land. Today, due to forced removal, the community resides in Northeast Wisconsin and is known as the Stockbridge-Munsee Community.

This book is for

Anne

(with an e)

A caricature, a swollen shadow,
A stupid clown of the spirit's motive,
Perplexes and affronts with his own darkness,
Delmore Schwartz, "This Heavy Bear that Goes with Me"

Let us try, if we can, to enter into death with open eyes.
last words of the Emperor Hadrian

CONTENTS

Prefatory Note

As I was putting this collection together I had a letter from an old friend. She remarked that we are called to "love what is wild and understand the power we do not have". I read that and thought of Saint Paul's "you are not your own"—a passage that has loomed across all my life and work.

The first wild things that moved me were the vacant lots in Queens (NYC), where I grew up. I made a story for myself about them—that a rubbished inhuman world had called the faustian world to build its monumental creatures so that, when Time's short spans struck them to ruin, the weeds and trash plants and bugs and lizards and snakes and birds nobody cared about—sparrows, starlings, pigeons, grackles—would thrive in the slow smokeless burning of the dead creatures that had left their makers behind. My most cherished figure for this was the sight of weeds growing in the concrete sidewalk cracks everywhere, slowly in their No Time breaking them down yet more completely. However romantic, those arose as precious scenes for me of an Innocence Abroad. And as I write this now I bless the absurdity of this elderly prose, even more romantic and chastening.

The second wild thing I encountered was the Latin Tridentine Mass. Called to serve as an Altar Boy was a prodigious and altering experience for an eleven year old, deranging all the senses, feelings, everything that was everyday, including the language you thought you were beginning to know. "The power we do not have" at work in the vacant lots was Nature's ministry, to be cherished as a secret and unsightly revelation. Swung low or sung high, the Latin Mass revealed Nothing. It was, and still is, an extravagant performance of "the power we do not have" that means to transact Nature and all forms of transnature, of which the Mass ritual is a longrunning undead instance.

The third wild thing with power we do not have came to me as poetry with its brave pledge of allegiance to "the necessity of art". My chief initial guides were Allen Ginsberg, Ogden Nash, and Marianne Moore—strange, but so it was. For more than twenty years they watched over me tracking across many foregone fairy lands. They eventually left me trying to make sense of the wild power that J. H. Prynne did not have—a wilderness mapped to the estranged coordinates of *Force of Circumstance* (1962) and *Kitchen Poems* (1968).

L=A=N=G=U=A=G=E—that timely stutterance—brought a measure of relief to my understanding of the necessity of art. Its anti-institutional enterprise fashioned sermons I took to heart because they were so resolutely discounted: "Air Heart" sermons, sometimes serious, often ludic, to be delivered among school children.

The power we do not have was spilling out of L=A=N=G=U=A=G=E's cracked and ruptured crucafflictions. "The necessity of art"? Here that stepped out as a last infirmity of those Aristocats born to the lost and found wilderness of enlightenment.

Nature and transnature are gifts of a power we do not have, poetry and verse acquirements that call those gifts to attention. That's why you can't do anything wrong if you try your hand at either. Many have written poetry who were, like myself, *not* poets—John Ruskin for instance, who wrote a great deal all his life. Unlike Ruskin, some few who were not poets—Dr. Johnson, Edward Fitzgerald—wrote poetry as fine as anything except the work of poetry's supreme masters. Ogden Nash sometimes wrote poetry but mostly he stayed with his excellent verse.

And then there is that special class of poets and versifiers—the Aristocats in steerage who took Nonsense on board. I am happy to report, with T. S. Eliot, that "death has undone so many" of them because there have always been so many of them out there, riddling away. The Scat Cats called to special attention here are Edgar Poe and Edward Lear, who once upon a time told so well the very same story this book tries to tell.

J.M.

The Cryptography of Edgar Poe

(after Stéphane Mallarmé)

As eternity translates him to himself at last
this poet slurs with a new kris
an epoch terrified at the unknown
death triumphing in that strangled voice.

They like a spastic mob having heard an angel
transport a jangled language into glory
loudly proclaim it all a witch's brew drunk
from a fouled contaminate concoction.

And if from that hostile earth and sky your wretched
hopes cannot erect a bogle fitte
to ornament the gorious tomb of Poe

the cryptic form of high hell-bent disaster
this stunned shape anyhow may lift a wall against
your looming pieties and profane expectorations.

I

This Is My Body

An Ax for the Frozen Sea

Weirdly and for ever rises up the rabble of the machines.
They multiply like rabbits, they come from the mills of generations,
                                        where are they going now?
Not to love, not to the factories of happiness.

Once again the men pour out, faithless and vain. Creation groans,
and love, too fit for them to give or to receive.
In an idiotic pride they think about the meaning of love
(they were closer to its truth when they worshipped cruel gods

and knew the nothing that belongs to men and to those gods).
The world has always served the sciences of the artificial
and was first possessed by stones anyhow too wise to speak any more.

Perverse men say the stones will speak again
                                        but they will not.
Do we dare escape in abandonment to the charm of impossible objects?
Adam spoke with beasts when they were very young.

Many now are dumb as brick or steel.
Others in a furious catastrophe hum or buzz, resisting wisdom.
Innocent birds or roaring lions willing or unwilling,
all shall come to have their tongues torn out, like saints.

To conceive this now stirs panic. Nonetheless, the machines, with men
                              are running out of time as quickly as possible.
They do not know this but they will.
Men of sympathy and imagination distrust the thought of their machines.

But there is no need, why be anxious, listen.
Do you hear the rust? Is somebody laughing at death?
The buildings are lost in silence when we have disappeared.

What are you holding onto after all? The world is free.
A fine dust is settling and the past awaits you.
When the winds vanish there is all that desolation.

Horizons watch the moveless flats,
the machines fall into starry darkness with no end in sight,
where love finds its place in this bewilderment.

Say nothing. Look, someone is playing.
Fire the mind point blank into the eye of the mind.
A black hole does not see and does not send. It holds the light.

Being With a Skin of Brain

The eyes go first, desperate for the gods they knew,
to flicker in a modest
way away. They are aversive to the Obsolete,
"I will not serve"
they say. Their faces fall, the watching faces ripple
like wax. Even the dullest
fear the eyes seeking the solution of this fire.
Colors striate, move

to grey, then greenish, yellow, the eyes turned and
finished gold. Messenger, now it is
the body's turn, the body
turns dust and water to a crystal suit of nerves.
No hand will touch

what once was flesh, the mind sets hard
acrylic. Nightmare by memory
the skull dissolves, the crust shrinks and runs,
wave after panicked
wave. Out of nowhere a dry metallic wind is shouting
commands, the bones
of the world pour out. Rabble and lucid black
thoughts grow
their final skin of brain, the steel electric
field of forms. What sense
remains of mind has fled to its extremities,
the fingers end and stiffen

into nails, driving teeth
hearing chewing stones
milling a way through dirt to air and
breath, spreading

discs of gold over legions at their brightening
silver edge,
zinc tongues, leather helmets, crying
fields, beating ancient banners.

Incidents in the Life of my Rebbe Virgil

(after Edward Lear)

1\.

When you travel Transterrania
(Should you ever have that mania)
"Thro' the silent hours of night",
If you turn a pirouette
Close your eyes and look — you bet!
It's my old pal Virgil Burnett,
(What's he reading? *Sein und Zeit*?)

2\.

No. But vatic and auratic
Beings, Byzantine or Attic,
Tore his hand and soul apart.
Teraphim in terra cotta,
Incubi, morgana fata
Chant enchanting incantata
And enspelled him into art.

3\.

Then his manner – slightly formal,
"Cool, collected", not your normal
Terran tourist. There are rumors
He had held discourse with cats,
Visited vast lunar flats
Watched wasp women's fierce combats —
Sights beyond this world's consumers.

4.

Lustral rites and lupanars
Long expunged from the Zohar;
    Mystics, fiends, saints — they'd delect his
Taste for images taboo,
Tainted texts he must construe.
He had tracked *les pas des loups*
    In banned books struck through with Xs.

5.

"What is pure? Find something purer,
Curious or curiouerer.
    If you quest for second sight".
This he said in shapely stories,
Inconvenient inventories,
And majestic gory glories —
    (What a fright for *Sein und Zeit*).

6.

O my Virgil, artful, old pal,
Lochinvar and Percival
    Played their day before the footlights
In their "lonesome latter years",
But the songs of gondoliers?
Or the Women of Algiers?
    (Out of sight in *Sein und Zeit*).

7.

They are hiding his abiding.
The lost rivers they are riding
    Run for ever out of sight,
Past the tomb of doomed King Arthur,

Through Ys, Mu, and lost Agartha,
Where men seek the Queen Astarte,
And the secrets of Siddhartha,
And the depthless eyes of Djaa.
        (Long forgot in *Sein und Zeit*).

Why I am not a Poet, I

(after Frank O'Hara)

I am not a poet, I am a pedant.
Why? I think I would rather be
a poet, but I am not. Well,
say my friend Jeffrey
is starting a poem. I drop in.
"Sit down and have a drink" he
says. We drink. I read. I look
up. "You have ANIMALS in it."
"Yes, it needed something there."
"Oh." I go and the days go by
and I drop in again. The poem
is going on, and I go, and the days
go by. I drop in. The poem is
finished. "Where's ANIMALS?"
All that's left is just
O, some letters. "It was too much."
But me? One day I am thinking of
a ballad of white swans. I research
about white swans. Pretty soon I see a
text and not just pages.
Page after page, there should be
so much more, of white swans and of
ballads and how dreadful white swans are
and life. Weeks go by, I am working day
and night, I am a scholar. My monograph
is finished and I've tracked down every
white swan known to man. It's called
A THEORY OF WHITE SWANS. Then one day in a book
I read his poem, called ANIMALS.

Voice or Verse or What

All afternoon I leave the open door
to talk you back to another masquerade of familiar
words our riddles in this conversation poem
                                        we are pretending

to be (seeing ourselves in some imaginary we,)
other characters in another story. I want you
(to forget our names, let us make up) I want you to
                                        make up my mind

like a face (another face for another place)
to face today. Let's suppose this is a poem
but you – where is that room of coded words
                                        (where I shall suppose

we live on parentheses some) where we are lying
together in a séance of faithless phrases and embedded
characters, betraying lust and various dangling
                                        constructions. What

are you (where are we borne from this poem, "in here")
what are you saying? ("where you at last see nothing,")
I can see your silver ring. I think I am beginning
                                        to see your silver ring.

The White Lady

"dying takes a special nerve
willing to seize that day
to self-inflict the theft of life"

she takes your breath away

II

from

Air Heart Sermons

Walls

Personally they take no sides
a wall is hard
a matter of indifference
a beginning of some sort anyway
they are built
they make a difference
for the ideal wall
has one side only in reality
like a ball
bearing what's impossible
to move around
the empires they have left behind
protect their own
depend upon it
if they had their way they would be white

Still they depend upon nothing
they need the ground
they will forget
in luxuries of air
walls must be upright to exist
as the writings on them say:
one thing
Jesus never walked on
about this
conflict is apparent
we have come to
possess much.

So neglectful of the ground
they make believe their own and call them floors
windows are dreams, doors are illusions.
        They finally fall down.

The Trial of Maldoror

He that is near me is near the fire.
Jesus, non-canonical saying

Our practice is to put the matter nicely
to labor in the truth you see but never mind
so let us put it right to you
the question a proposal the screws maybe
    you can't tell
    what speak what judge what revelation
    these labyrinths you say are hell.

Our devices are like you naturally innocent
of meaning any harm you get by heart
here at least love recalls the inquisition of your pleasures
where life is short and art is long all craft is punishment
    and you can't tell
    what speak what judge what revelation
    why this labyrinth they say is hell.

And anyway you take us more or less
princes of darkness   psychopaths reserved
go straight turn left right whatever doesn't matter
you can't escape this emptiness
    nor could you ever tell
    why speak what judge what revelation
    let's say these labyrinths are hell.

Again a day

Again a day dawns breaking the code of silence

But he mustn't
Look here we are
Written backwards now
The end comes quickly
So quick the dead
New paper "silver wheels"

Night is failing again
A day dawns breaking the code of silence

The Return of the Irrelevant Proverbs

Surround yourselves   in the imaginary   the words
of the   we know   nothing   real
as fire is to much   to ask and to desire
cracks   that spread
sudden   tangled   lines upon the placid   surfaces
like some crazy   blip   a weakneed syntax
for those lines of   for the   unapparent   what to
exterminate   flee to the   edges drop off
clear   the way   into the inner   spaces beyond   borders
here   perhaps where   stones begin to slur
motions to the unsuspecting   air
presses on   this heavy dearthly   emptiness
comes casually   out of print   confused   sounds
dream away   their lines   trust
to ignorance   all your own
happiness   that makes the heart afraid   and lies

Air Heart Sermon

Where are the   arbitrary and transubstantial   forums form
above   shapeshifting   futures   the stone
spreading   the complex silence   gathering   around
itself   unconcerned with any   parts of speech
braking for   something sometime   feelings flee
to salvage   daydreams too   far away
listen   enter   the park of   possibilities
the mazes of   the breathless   drift to
          to cerebrate   to lift a toast   to death

Dead End

somewhere else in the knotworks of his brain
he listens for a distance throbbing low and in repeating
turns of rhythm. He went for it, until it seemed
though he had lost his way I knew a place to go
drawn by an end nowhere in sight but wholly in sound.
If God laid the world out on an anvil
and the blows beat out like Blake, infinity
would rush up howling in your face to face
their final turn and that Enormous Room
and the deafening sound of machines bolted firmly to cement
turning great wheels in heavy steel cylinders.
Noise at that superlative becomes a place
where you could see far at the end a door
if you were to go on would you open it
if you knew you would understand at last
"simply everything"? That is where ambition stops:
"To become immortal, then to die". Those words
were on that door he'd never open.

The Foetus that Devoured Cleveland

He is all the men I ever knew
including me, and all the women too

The evidence of things not seen,
love (so we said) betrayal (what we mean)

Deliberate as Jesus, meaner than this poem
my odd illusion   Vanity begins at home

A life pursuit of liberty and evil and
happiness the foetus that devoured Cleveland

Proverbs drop a truth that lights the mind
In that fire each burns after his own kind.

How and Why to End the World, I, II

I.

The beautiful   inclines   to last   surrenders
to our minds   delight   in   puzzles
refuse   what gods have joined   in   violence   together
surfaces   and limits   even   will   empty   reflections
on the common   place   form   a last judgment
amounts   to   nothing   will   appear   to   light
like   wise   apparitions   can   be   counted   on
to many   purposes   deliver   the end
in sight   out of its mind   diagrams   reform
all   our words   design   what we hold   on   to
wind   down   the evidence of things not seen   by
the imaginations   of   men's hearts   continually   evil

II.

the dreams images corrupt the dreams
images corrupt the dreams images
corrupt the dreams images corrupt
the dreams images corrupt the dreams

progress only desires progress
only desires progress only
desires progress only desires
progress only desires progress

the mind itself releases the mind
itself releases the mind itself
releases the mind itself releases
the mind itself releases the mind

Adolescent Images

Enter my life
like a piano only
asking to be played

I will get to know you
like a book you will be still
more mysterious

And forgive the execution of my passion
when I have you in my mind
I behave badly

and understand
my sex object my purity my silence
when you speak I know you never speak to me.

Primitive Calculus

Such a mistake to want
Clarity above all things.
Louise Gluck, "Moonless Night"

First above all things is clarity
then comes darkness
then the light
where we know
                                        where we know
no law at the limit of knowing
velocities of vision
the hard extremes of pleasure
beyond
unbreathable
stars

Ivy, Virginia, September 11, 2011.

On this day we repeat our precedents of fear.
A Documentary Transcription

Audisne haec Amphiarae sub terram abdite?
Sophocles, *Epigoni*

DIALOGUES OF THE DEAD

"Death
Is here. Up to the field, and give
Away thy breath."

"This morning in a field near Shanksville Pennsylvania,
in a vast stretch of grassland
("There is a field, of many, one" …
the poet Robert Pinsky
"speak of something that is gone")

read out the names of forty people
"but not the Canaanites"

speak of something that is gone

this morning   of many, one
near   shady   travelers   (haunt)   "among Arabian sands"
something is gone
the names   both of them speak   of   people
"completely forget"

"That morning in a small motel near
("Why linger, why turn back, why shrink, my heart")

"Pray the morning prayer in a group and ponder the great rewards of that prayer. Make supplications afterwards, and do not leave your apartment unless you have performed ablution before leaving, because the angels will ask for your forgiveness as long as you are in a state of ablution, and will pray for you."

"They shopped at Walmart, ate at Denny's....
"Don't worry, Dad.... It will be quick.
Flight 175, Flight 11, Flight 77, Flight 93,
follow where all is fled

A HISTORY OF *THE TWO TOWERS*

"the five senses, the chief inlets of Soul in this Age"

"The profound moral failures of the age of 9/11 belong to the murderers of Al Qaeda, and those (especially in certain corners of the Muslim clerisy, along with a handful of bien-pensant Western intellectuals) who abet them, and excuse their actions. The mistakes we made were sometimes terrible (and sometimes, as at Abu Ghraib and in the CIA's torture rooms, criminal) but they came about in reaction to a crime without precedent."

Forgive us our trespasses
Prepare slaughter for his children for the iniquity of their fathers
crime without precedent
Wilmington North Carolina, November 10, 1898. This morning in the
Light Infantry Armory near
Death Camps *without precedent*
Napituca...Gnadenhütten ...Bad Axe...Bloody Island... Indian Island...
Bear River...Marias...Wounded Knee,

The profound moral failures
Sodom........Amalek............Jericho.................Jabesh-Gilead...
Mystic ... (crime without precedent) ... the Land of Canaan
Melos...Kristallnacht... Deir Yassin...Srebrenica...Darfur
of the Age

completely forget the world
the flesh
the devil
of 9/11
"the mindless hatred...thousands...Americans"

"Sing us one of the songs of Zion"
1. By the rivers of Babylon we sat and wept when we remembered
Zion ...
8. Daughter of Babylon, doomed to destruction, happy is the one who repays you, according to what you have done to us.
9. Happy is the one who seizes your infants and dashes them against the rocks.

" Do you know what I see? I see that God alone has become everything. Men and animals are only frameworks covered with skin, and it is He who is moving through their heads and limbs. I see that it is God Himself who has become the block, the executioner, and the victim for the sacrifice." He fainted with emotion.... "Pain", he consoled them again, "is unavoidable".

Ramakrishna, January 1, 1886

"A light is passed from the revolving year"

On that bright morning EST (it is) it was still dark in Los Angeles, where on the road to the hospital a young contagious man was dying, a cocaine framework covered with skin. His friend watched his slow motion life in horror ("we all watched in horror") as he flew toward death. Why linger, why turn back? But he did, though the planes did not, since the West Coast attendants insisted. A

single call to that other time (EST) left a message hanging in dead
air. The telephone networks were clogged with death.

"9/11? I remember", she remembered ("no one asked what she
remembered – who knew? They remembered only Zion").
"He was dying
in Los Angeles and we couldn't talk to him or to anyone there. A
single message – call waiting — and then silence. ("Don't worry,
Dad. It will be quick.") No phones, no flights. He was dying
by himself. People watched in horror at the planes, everyone
came together, stunned, whispering ("no one could believe it").
I couldn't watch, we couldn't talk. There he was ("of many, one"),
in Los Angeles, and here I was (EST) in Ivy Virginia, looking at the
rich empty field behind the house, a small stretch of lush meadow
that badly needed bushhogging."

NEGATIVE SPACE

"The unconditional renunciation of consolation"
Theodore Adorno

Hilton Head Island, South Carolina. 11 September 2011. In Commemoration of the 10th anniversary of September 11, 2001, the Hilton Head Choral Society will present a musical tribute to the heroes, victims and survivors of the terrorist attacks that forever changed our nation.

"but not the Canaanites"

This special performance, titled "Songs of Consolation and Hope," is the second event of Hilton Head Island's oldest performing arts organization's 36th season. This concert has been specially designed to bring our community together to remember the past, celebrate the present and look forward to a future filled with creativity, imagination and peace

that forever changed our nation ("… the many change and pass")

traditional annunciation of consolation
the conclusion of *The Book of Job* 42: 10-17

10. And the Lord turned the captivity of Job, when he prayed for his
friends: also the Lord gave Job twice as much as he had before.
11. Then came there unto him all his brethren, and all his sisters,
and all they that had been of his acquaintance before, and did eat bread
with him in his house: and they bemoaned him, and comforted him over
all the evil that the Lord had brought upon him: every man also gave him
a piece of money, and every one an earring of gold.
12. So the Lord blessed the latter end of Job more than his beginning: for
he had fourteen thousand sheep, and six thousand camels, and a thou-
sand yoke of oxen, and a thousand she asses.
13. He had also seven sons and three daughters.
14. And he called the name of the first, Jemi'ma; and the name of the sec-
ond, Kezi'a; and the name of the third, Keren–hap'puch.
15. And in all the land were no women found so fair as the daughters of
Job: and their father gave them inheritance among their brethren.
16. After this lived Job a hundred and forty years, and saw his sons,
and his sons' sons, even four generations.
17. So Job died, being old and full of days.

Peace of Resistance

(thoughts of Gramsci)

> *"Prison is so finely wrought a file*
> *that, tempering one's thought,*
> *it makes of it a style."*
>
> ("a certain [Carlo] Bini")

"Was Bini really in prison? Perhaps
not for very long. Prison is so
finely wrought a file that it destroys

thought utterly." And he would know.
What is immortal in the mind are walls
thrown up only to be battered slowly

back to the ruth and rubble of the flesh
with gout and Pott's disease and stabbing
unheroic breaks full of bourgeois maladies
"acute gastric disorders" grubbing
their share of pain, tubercular chest,
angina and sclerotic arteries pumping
like an old man uphill on a bike. Rest
is what he needed, not to be dead
and resurrected in a book full of shit,

"the measure of history" he called to mind
when he had his bad dreams and his fill
of Bini's poem, and when he said

that prison was a file wrought so finely
it wore the mind to live down "like the master
craftsman who received a trunk of finely

seasoned olive wood with which to carve
a statue of St. Peter. He carved away

a piece here, a piece there.

He shaped the handsome wood roughly
modified it, corrected it, and watched fall
as the work of his hands only

the smooth handle of a cobbler's awl".

Bats Clinging in the Eaves

hanging around

bats

you may hear

clinging

"lovely bell-like notes" somewhere
deep

in the eaves

thinking after thoughts

waiting

for the light

to be over

thrown and past them

creaking

a way

through the darkness

III
Scientific Animals

Scientific Animals

Even the dead remember living a little
                                        strengthless heads
float in indoor avenues
                                        consumed in a music
of consuming. If they could eat through glass
                                        they would   they would
find a way. The movie of their eyes
                                        drools like a river.
It isn't love they want, these animals
                                        moving in a final fire,
poor lust to purer lovers who are dying in a face.

And then the gangs of silver, the wild
                                        mechanical dogs
loping to the days of carnival. Ring or
                                        wristband, snakeskin
slaughterers of innocence, who is left to
                                        prey upon? This fluid
dust, small silver, this small change of
                                        flesh that once was
grass, that once was grass?

Pasadena Ca. Nov. 3, 1983, 5:15 p.m.

As the eyes grow cool now descend immortal
soul into this darkening view of earth. The bright
empire of air tilts into air and dies,
the play of light turns on a revenant spool,
it is taking your breath away into the night,

it is the briefest space of time. A hand throws
the sky against a wall, a spillway of blue runs
off. The dry wash of light floods swiftly
down to the horizon's glimpse of fire, the rose
and spread of dust hanging between the thermonuclear sun

we do not see and the immobilized products of earth they
do. They are putting down their tools, everyone
stops, heads lifted through the dark listening
to the heat and uproar of the figures, their celebrations dying
for ever into colors, forms, and finally the one
blackness of forgetting. What we are is what they say.

The Man in the Red Crowned Hat

(for G. B. M.)

there is no necessity for labour and its
products to assume a fantastic form different
from their reality. They take the shape, in the
transactions of society, of services in kind and
payment in kind.

Karl Marx, *Capital* I.4

The man sits at a draughting board, his ears
are plugged
in black cups to a private music. He is drawing
a world
to his desire through atoms of tense incoherent
light.

The images stand in the vacuum of his eyes,
he finds
escape is possible. He wears a white cap bearing
Celtic
words in gothic lettering. The crown is red. Greek
characters

declare themselves in European shapes, black on a
plain white
ground. On the brim's brightness shadowing dark eyes
is a date
published in bold arabic numbers. The time is
the present.

Today his interest is consumed in figures of commerce
and industry,
where nothing will be real, where all is made subject
to high

imaginations, polished surfaces, and finished forms,
and money.

In his hands money will talk, mechanical
instruments
will learn and teach the living he will make. He
abandons
himself to translation, people evanescing into
these

perfect things. A chromeplated revolver hovers
nowhere,
its parts at peace: hollow barrel touches the
cylinder's
cool cosmetic skin and nothing happens. Bullet, pin,
and trigger

find a patience drawn to perfection, to this
weapon's
balanced wooden grip. Elsewhere other impossible
machines
and pieces of machines are waiting to reproduce,
advertisements

in themselves. They live to sell themselves. The man
in the red
crown cap vends the desires, his alphabets are
imagined,
a faultless box of cigarettes, giant zipper, Logos.
An exploded

TDK cassette is rising to depart in perfect order and
detail.
Later this afternoon the man in the red crown
cap will
listen to its borrowed artificial soul. He will find
himself

seated at his draughting board, his ears still
                                        plugged
in black cups to a private music. He keeps drawing the
                                        world
to his desire through atoms of tense incoherent
                                        light.

Sieve

The soul's life begins in dark revulsion, a first flight past the consolations of unhappiness. You are hollowed out with purpose, you must imagine you will never sin again.

Set out at once upon a 6 x 6 foot slab of plywood. Fix it somewhere you can see and think about. Now you are ready to computate your sins. Rule 1: at each day's end go to the board and drive a nail for every sin you sinned that day. You will be your soul's cartographer. It is your project till death do its part.

Rule 2: If – do not say "when" – a sinless day should pass, that day take one nail from the board. You are tracking the mathematical enormity of evil and its laws of form. Once you walked in darkness, now you see into a deeper darkness. In the miraculous days to come, in sinless days that receive their strict recording, you will be moving through galvanic power, like an automaton.

Gripped by God, you glimpse from time to time the promise of an absence of nails. You are working out a set of arithmetical problems. You are still in elementary school. You are a good student.

One day the miracle will have been accomplished. Reaching to remove a nail you discover none, the absence of the nails in a field of black splintered holes.

This absence has a name, "the temporal punishment due to sin". Your sins are forgiven, poured out and purified through the sieve you made yourself.

Could you fill those holes, sand the board smooth, perhaps overpaint it? The vanity of an imagination that is evil continually, a rich and faintly comical economy of grace. Your spiritual life's Advancement of Learning has run out of a badly printed book to seek an Aral Sea. You have weighed yourself and found yourself wanting.

The Loves of the Machines

The night comes   on   one   seeking   first
a book   and then   an absence
of a man   not yet   together
as the dying   part   their playing   promises
adjust him   otherwise
he begins to learn   apace
a space   a world   he never   fades
out   he believes   the waste   again
turns blue   prints   for the possible
and old despair   ends   cross
purposes   too   soon

to begin   this   then   is not
enough   when but for the grace of
what   goes back to love   and   nothing   else
where for the time being   altogether
warped   into quiet   opportunities   arise
where   these   circles
never end   this way
lies   madness   must be   simple
puzzles   or   functions   sufficiently well
organized senses   the mind   can take   over and above
the gods are   what   they overthrow

these   are   the loves
of the machines   we know nothing   of
the end   they have   in mind   for us
the fear   of love
sentences   betrayals
so complete   we will be   alone   the memory of
death   to the invaders

Met a Language

They are clearly difficult
in every sense
machines metallic to
the tongue
the g
listening eye
dispersed
throughout
(the body of a poem) openly ly
ing about itself the feel
full of folk the truth
snared caught and taken in
(the body of falsehood,
the house of life)

Aenigma: An Image

(in a Game)

by amor's jungle i wcpt xvjdzhkq

I
m mediate
first principle, atomic
figure in hiding
still whirled in this
this literal mist, invisible (Lucreti-
an image
in avoidance
tiny bits playing
their music
evening voluntaries, little hesitations
in this middle beginning
it is   within without
it is
in this instrumental equation
"Neti, Neti"
distinct thin imprinted   it is in
simply being
gifts divinity Venice
in ruins   begins again, light
similarities, mists, whirlwinds
spin its units, splitting
time springing winter into   arctic   action   aquamarine
chinas pakistanis in foreign legions
spin
fingal finger final spin
this initial series is
ice city lion discourse >PRINT
thick misspell files >PRINT disaster devotion >PRINT
>PRINT this i instinct in light

N

or ought one

imagine an exponential finale
not anything, something definite and then
unsaid and then, envisioning subtraction
not now Nagarjuna's emptiness, now
an emptying into
journeys joinings evenings
never Being (apparitions) again divisions, only
haunted, never in "what is here you I
this love" names instead signs in
("not this, not that")
visiblings and absent "from all that seems to
matter" women men things an "Indianan image"
moving and disappearing
turning negative and necessary, burn and now (new)
know(ing) not (knot) knowledge (entropy) under
privileged another strength another hands finger
pointing touching another hand reaching and enduring
in silence now another kingdom borne
down another burning
Sous le soleil de Satan.

A

lexical

Astarte, entertaining
that day's wraith's
flames falling, Alph-
an images, textual acrobatic
daimons — topaz, breathless agate, air. Death
arrives speaking mathematically:
intermedia, adorable
invasive apparition scrap
paper shards arise again as
black as tar te-
nacious, invariant, a last or-

acle plastic as beauty vanishing a-
mazed, littoral as law

G
host allows ash love loss
(the absinthe of these lines the)
imagined "Genius locus"
ingrained engulphed
not like ourselves mortal but with the faces of
gods, transcending, general, being-in-itself
(but??)
needing something (else to)
get along
(too too?) gripped (to) things (to) living
things, morning songs angels
themselves-
selving, recording
angels, gods gripped (by) being
(not to dust, devoted, never yet borne
to the) "daughters of men", forgetting reigns (of)
light remembering evening descending
(like the earth but truly)
Gea, something having gripped Agean
image, angels, gods, "the green world"
running (how)
strange (it all seems)

A
my gate mica
muse che
lights me, stonish
sexual
maze like
gaze
drift ural, fire
verse

blaze
more logical
stray scribe live
lone star-
te
flame
better men

M
emory
migrations, magic dumps, metal murmuring
"i treni transsiberiani magente"
thumpa thumpa thumpa thumpan
image. Mobile numbers, summon somewhere
music, numbing sermons. Magellan's whimsical
embracing magic — amorous Moroccan
zombies stumble, impale themselves;
immense motors , "miserere nobis" — impinge, impel
implode. Phantom, "implora pace". Madden,
atomize my mind , minimize imbruted
thumb, moth, morning, primitive miracles
monstrance, metonym, mortification. Hangman,
imbecile — come, dismember, rhyme.

E
nd-chanter
"beautiful ineffectual angel"
unseen Are Yellow multitudes winged
Each azure the feed hear
steep leaves Heaven spread aery
the even zenith's the sepulchre
fire The Lulled pumice towers
overgrown sense powers The sapless
suddenly hear bear power less
be Heaven Scarce thee wave
heavy like lyre are deep

fierce Drive Like the Ashes
trumpet behind
                                        breath the like
hectic their where corpse the
earth everywhere whose like shed
Angels blue Like some verge
The be congregated waken Mediterranean
crystalline Baiae's the flowers whose
themselves the the tremble dead
thee The uncontrollable comrade when
ne'er sore the chained tameless
the The tone Be dead
withered verse Be prophecy West
presence driven pale
chariotest seeds
like sister dreaming hues hear
loose are Ocean the surge head
the height year Vaulted hear
blue the isle Quivering azure
them Cleave sea-blooms foliage fear
were were share free The
then seemed prayer leaf weight
thee even like tone Be
dead withered verse Be prophecy
                                        being leaves Enchanter red
bed they grave Her sweet
Destroyer stream earth's the there
surface the fierce the the Ode
the whose summer where streams
sleep wave's sweet the while
wear ocean despoil leaf wave
impulse even wanderings skiey have
need life bowed Make forest
harmonies sadness impetuous the quicken
unextinguished earth comes

IV
Transubstantiations

Though heavyweathered magamen
Should march up from their fen again
To harass guys and dolls again,
They then shall turn hasbeenagain.

from Edward Gorey,
The Gory Allegories [unpublished]

A Set for Edward Lear and Lewis Carroll

The Ballad of the Vast Invention Tree

1.
In a Land Transoceanic
Past the vast Immensett Sea,
By the river Twaddlequiver
Rose the great Invention Tree,
Guarded in a garden closely
By Lord Luminosity.
In serapes and sarongs,
There the Bos and Nims and Quongs
Grow up pictures, poems, and songs,
In the Land Transoceanic
Past the vast Immensett Sea.

2.
Ages ancient and posterior
Hid in beatific bowers,
Stirred a Vision Bird to tell of
Flagrant hands with dreamy powers
Flicking flakes of fragrant showers
Hours and hours on vagrant flowers.
"'T is our Being Beatific
(Sang the Bird in tones terrific)
Our amazing beatific
Lady Luminosity
Lady Luminosity."

3.
But on Isolation Island
Ruled the demons Don't and Never,
Among rocks and scrubby sages
Skinny characters and clever
Fixing number, weight, and measure,

To translate and name that treasure
With their strict insistency,
That creation of the Lady,
The Impossabilla Tree
Skinny demons Don't and Never
Dried-up demons Don't and Never!

4.
Lady blively, magic, sainted,
Scans her land majestically
"Would that once upon our Wood Land
Grew a great Invention Tree!"
Trochees straight turn anapaestics
Wood Lands dream of hypermetrics,
(Don't and Never turn dyspeptics –
"Rhymes and lines are running free!")
"Homonymphs and Synonymphies
Call the Dimplies and the Simplies
And the Smarties and the Pimplies
Para no masiacly
Para no messiacly."

5.
Then the little letters lightly
Litter light along those lawns,
While the long are lighting out for
Limpid glimpses of that dawning
Where the Funny Nims, reborn,
Watch the Silly Belles of morning,
Lyric ladies, ludic, lisping,
Unheard melodies are listing —
All the nymphs are unresisting
Where the long and little letters
Lightly lisp along the lawn.

6.
"What? a Would Land in a Wood Land,
And some Village,— Though or Maybe?
Simply squishy, suppositious."
All things special and propitious,
Weather wishous or delicious
They pronounced both mad and vicious.
"Bonny burdies and absurdies
Spinning tunes on hurdy-gurdies
We transform to dirty wordies" –
Bonny burdies and absurdies,
Happy tunes on hurdy-gurdies.

7.
So 'mid rocks and scrubby sages
Shrinking from those winds of whims,
These crazed demons take to shouting
"Silly Belles and Phoney Nims
Do not multiply yours sims,
Here are Information Hymns!
Border ballads of disorder,
Siren songs on Pan's recorder –
Bad words — Silence! — come to order!
Here are Information Hymns,
Hear our Information Hymns."

8.
Demon dumbsters Don't and Never
Dance a puppet pantomime,
Faster masters of disasters
Raining ruin out of time
Growing rich in runic crime
Through this coo-coo clock of rhyme.
All the simplies and the dimplies,
All the smarties and the pimplies,
Look and giggle at your disease

Demon dumbsters caught for ever
In this coo-coo clock of rhyme.

9.
And the Funny Nims inflected,
(Clearly here the spell they're under)
List the Lady's ludic lisping,
While the Lord of mimic thunder
Shook the Silly Belles asunder,
Turning all that world to wonder
At a Lady sailing hither
Shedding starlight like that river,
Called the noble Twaddlequiver –
Lady Luminosity!
Lady Luminosity!

10.
Past the Land Transoceanic,
Past the vast Immensett, — See!
Demons turn to Demon Lovers
At the great Invention Tree,
Singing "Beatific Lady,
We have come here to be free."
    Then the Bos and Nims and Quongs
    Show how synonymphy songs
    Sung to homophonic gongs
    Can set time to run for ever
    In this coo-coo clock of rhyme.

The Legend of the Vast Invention Tree

Far away in the Land of Lovely Language the world is ruled by the Lord and Lady Luminosity. Here Fabled Creatures live happily ever after in the song of a Vision Bird, who dwells once upon a time in his secret ancient home. There he sings a neverending song to the glory of the Lady Luminosity. So pleasing is the Vision Bird's song to the Lady and her Lord that their happiness radiates across the world to All the Fabled Creatures. When the Fabled Creatures join this song, the face of the world turns to the Land of Lovely Language.

And when in that once upon a time two Fabled Creatures took a turn to face away, the luminous world turned outside in and cast up Isolation Island, near whose deep romantic chasm arose a dark Impossibilla Tree. And then no birds began to sing their unheard melodies.

And when that island's Nonsongs drifted down that vale of tears, the Lady Luminosity, listing to their birdless songs, unheard the melodies of the Impossible Would Land she had always known. Then it was that the Invention Tree appeared in its greatest glory out of a secret fractal covert, turning all the world to wonder at the neverending magic of the Impossible Would Land. And ever since, in the Land Transoceanic, the world is music everywhere.

When can her glory fade?
O the wild change she made!
All the world wonder'd.
Honour the change she made!
Wordly and light brigade,
Noble and number'd!

The Wordor of Nott

He writes Won't and Don't, No and Never a lot,
The Wordor of Nott.

Is he sad or bad? Is he sick? Is he mad?
Does he miss his Mom? Did he lose his Dad,
                                        or WHAT's
                                        with the Wordor of Nott?

Was he poor at sports? No friends at school?
What secret explains his Non Serviam rule,
                                        this DESPOT
                                        ical Wordor of Nott?

Or is he enspelled by some sick antique dream
Of Astarte, and Djaa, and that flash lass Faustine,
                                        the HARLOT
                                        of the Wordor of Nott?

Why would anyone sail in a sieve to Cockayne?
DNA? The I Ching? The dark mark of Cain?
                                        the TAROT,
                                        or the ordures of Nott?

A star chart? A bottle of Ring-Bo-Ree?
The Jade Books? The Zohar? Libri Sibyllini?
                                        THE DAUGHTERS OF LOT?
                                        Oh Sir Wordor, say not.

You ensembles of chipmunks offending my ears,
You subsuperheroes on cartoon careers,
                                        REQUIESCAT.
                                        I'm the Wordor of Nott,

No more Good Guys and Bad Guys and other dumb things!
We set sail for a world where the fat Lady sings
MEGAWATT
as the Wordor of Nott.

O Eve, O Madam, in Eden I'm Adam,
O keep faith with our cryptogrammatical infam
ous PLOT
and the Wordor of Nott.

For those Silly Belles synonymphonical rhymes
Run a discourse discobbled from linguistic crimes
POLYGLOT,
like the Wordor of Nott.

If you think when a Nowhere turns Somewhere is queer
Déjà vous to discover it's (presto!) now here
UNBEGOT
by the Worder of Nott.

Rare Amanda the Queen, Ogden Nash, Edgar Guest,
Whose muses your conscience inclines to detest
but CANNOT,
for the Wordor of Nott

Found the vacancy bent on absorbing its space
Where all fixedness somehow sideslips out of place,
the MARPLOT,
of the Wordor of Nott.

Alcatraz, Devil's Island, or famous Santé,
Where that Good Thief of God, the rad fag Jean Genet,
hits the SPOT
of the Wordor of Nott,

Where angels performing invisible vigils
Dance their doggerel dazzle and quizzable sigils
as HOT
as the Wordor of Nott.

At that imageless point of degree writing zero
Stands the imperfect godlike enklupzified hero
a SOT
like the Wordor of Nott,

And the boy still sings on the burning deck
Of the meaningless wreck of the Odradek
the UPSHOT
of the Wordor of Nott.

You must summon that engine the world's rarely seen
Be the being who lived just to build that machine,
— no ROBOT
of the Wordor of Nott,

An Infernal Negation exacting contraption
Making calls upon Nothing to sing into action,
or NOT
says the Wordor of Nott.

For the world is a pangram that each must compose,
And it maps to the Nothing that Nobody Knows
— the ARGOT
of the Wordor of Nott.

Poe's poems and prose, like the emperor's clothes,
Are undressed to the Nothing that Nobody Knows,
the JACKPOT,
of the Wordor of Nott.

For Nothing observed that American Girl
Called The Mythical force more reNOvates the world,
this we WOT,
says the Wordor of Nott.

O is or will or was begot
a Wordor of Nott?

The Klupzies

1.

He stares and stares through the dawn all day,
Every night at a quarter to three,
From the poop at the fantail he feels the wind
With a message that says he's a man destined
　　　　Toward the kingdom Beondweesie.
"Beondweesie, Beondweesie!
That's a word, not a world," they all laugh "Tee hee!"
Who take their stand on the land at hand,
Never hearing what he hears – that higher command.
　　　　That he drives on assiduously.
Once a pair, one's not there –
Why socks disappear, who knows?
Don't despair if they're off somewhere
In the playground of missing clothes.

2.

He knows where he goes he should follow his nose,
　　　　By night at a quarter past nine,
Past the submarine groves of the fantail plants
Where once sunk the City of Underpants
　　　　Near the hot equatorial line.
No compass, no quadrant, no message, no map,
No iphone, no ipad, no kindle, no app,
Could ever make contact or hope to detect
(If you try you will find you'll get perfectly wrecked)
　　　　This strange ship's undiscovered design.
Once a pair, one's not there –
Why a sock would be free, who knows?
To play solitaire? vanish into thin air?
At the playground of missing clothes?

3.
But on days forlorn there's the unseen storm
Like a spitting and upreared cat!
For the dog star went raging beside the moon,
So she turned to a howling and dark typhoon –
With her barnacled baseball bat!!
Her eyes peer over the pitching sea
Like a banshee seeking to spree debris.
Then her numberless murmuring mermen bestride
Her looming waves — and oh, woe betide!
That frumious Tiamat!
Once a pair, one's not there —
Why a sock would be free, who knows?
Perhaps it's feeling a *mal de mer*
Or an absence of missing clothes.

4.
And beware if the nixies fall quiet by night,
As you ride in your *poupe de ville*,
For the siren's silence surpasses, men say,
Their Sicilian songs, or a fish fillet
Served fresh from a charcoal grill.
Not that cryptid shore (Yacumama's door)
Nor all the gore of the Trojan War,
Strikes greater fear in your inner ear —
Not an unoiled gear nor a bombardier,
Nor the thrill of a dentist's drill.
Once a pair, now lost and rare
Has it slipped to a sleepy repose
In the *laissez faire* of a rocking chair
Dreaming of yesteryear's snows?

5.
But if you fare forth with an air debonaire
Through these monstrous and visible spaces
The hydra, leviathan, ningen, and kraken,

From their dreams of destruction will swiftly awaken
                    And appear as most risible faces.
Gold lightning, green grass, blue ice and red fire
Spread wide in this landscape their wings of desire,
And the paces and pauses of wild klupzy feet
Sound as footfalls of angels in alley and street
                    In palatial poetical places.
Once a pair, don't despair
Search the City of Underpants!
(Unexposed to the grownups of Vanity Fair)
For the playland of off-rhymed chance!

6.
There the steep stars stare through the all day dawn
                    Past the moon of the quarter to be,
From the poop at the fantail we follow the wind
Past a passage that leads to this land destined
                    To the klupzies' Beondweesie.
Beondweesie where the klupzies be,
Where a world's in the words, — just come and see!
Take a love craft boat, bring a fishing line,
Paint a color out of space, draw a moment out of time,
It's as easy as A B C.
Prickly pair, wear and tear,
When a sock goes free (we repeat)
It has found a *frère* (perhaps Fred Astaire)
In a Roseland of happy feet.

Ballad of a Dream in Demons

(A Fragment)

"Cast in this fastness, a fateful pair
What can we do now, what do we dare?
Our empty room has gobbled all
Those floral coral melodies
Drifting in mysterious trees
Where elphins shower and fairies fall
Past the vast Immensett Seas.

"And as we draw our outside in,
The afrits, marids, angels and the djinn
Will never praise our supernatural sighs,
Or make us laugh with fright,
At some bright uprisen sprite
With her rainbow-raining effervescent eyes,
Fancy fitful Fly-by-night."

The Howl of the Copycat

1.
The howl of the copycat few dare hear
Who think nothing's new under the sun.
All flesh is grass and like leaves of glass
We scatter the stars for fun.
What one calls *The Dipper*, to others 's *The Plough*,
Ursa Major, *Saptarishi*, *Charles' Wain*.
From Bilbao to Macao every cat says *Meow*!
Day and night follows morning again
and again
and again
Day and night follows morning again.

2.
His, hers, yours and mine, we all want to rhyme,
Since as Image and Likeness we're kin,
We use mirrors of words to abuse what's absurd,
It's perhaps our Original Sin.
The Good King Haroun (who can carry a tune
On his true counterfeit counter-feet)
As he treads plenilune through that Palace of Hoon
The refrain of this song will repeat
And repeat
And repeat,
"The brain of this song is complete."

3.
Just as everyone's face radiates its own grace,
(Take Alice Liddell's, if you like!)
Wonderlands are interred in each minim chauffeured in
La meme, *parecidos*, and *gleich* .
In Batak , in Telugu, in Uzbek and Bantu,
Deutsch, English, Francais, Espagnole,

Like the poets from Chengdu, they all do their voodoo —
When they howl out their copycat souls
their souls
their souls
The Tao of their copycat's soul.

The Nothing that Nobody Knows

When the mutant music of morning spills
Across these mute inglorious hills,
        And the heartsick scorpion crawls
And the eager eagles cry
As they beat at the desolate sky
        (Oh feeble wings! Ah forbidden walls!)
As the angels of God zip by

(Those missioned minions from antique dominions,
Like vacant Virginians with silly opinions).
        Then a lethal thunder unknown to that tundra
Rolled on like a raving mad
Cyclonic byronic jihad
        Of a creature committed to standing misunder
And singing this freak ballade:

"My brain's not sane, I need champagne,
A gravy train, or a capital gain!
A glass of sherry or canzonieri
I could write and mail to the Virgin Mary,
Beseeching her grace for a personal loan
Or a ticket to skip to Sierra Leone."
Oh! Is this the cock that crowed in the morn
        His forlorn torchsong
For the Akond of Swat and *La Mort de Marat*,
        A long Monophthong,
For a lost and forgotten Dada?

Yes, hear that awful dole
        ful hymn of that polar zone
Like a geek who schleps through bituminous steppes
        (Oh that groan of an overthrown clone!)
Where the scoriac rivers that run up Mount Yaanek
Once led the Dark Bard (nevermore in a panic)

To Ululand's ultimate goal
To croon to a moon alone.
And all the woods and valleys ran
With an omen that no men knew part of a plan –
"Breathe the air of this lune de clair!
Search the City of Underpants!
(Unexposed to the grownups of Vanity Fair
'Tis the playland of off-rhymed chance!"

"That intense inane! Oh sing it again,"
Wailed the boys from their desolate shore,
"Sing the guys and dolls and the great *noir* molls
And Niagara Falls, and the tuvan calls
As they summon the angel Lenore."
And list to the gargles and skaldic warbles,
The heart-wrung ringing of near and far bells
From a poet once thought to have lost his marbles
Through the mental strain of the rain in Spain,
Or from being too fain of the whooping crane.
So the boys turned their eyes from that lost horizon's
Extinct pigeons and thunderous bison
To quest after Grpljx and Sparse Infectors,
And the Bfrifs in flight from the virus protectors!
Yet the songs of that grand and forsaken shore
Are swooning and crooning as ever before,
"Once so fair, where's the there?
Where the Bots would be free to suppose?
Perhaps they've sunk in a *mal de mer*
Dreaming of yesteryear's snows."

Thus an awful darkness and silence arose
Across that besimulate land,
Like a cheese soufflé or that bubbly prose —
"Like when", "Like say"—like, bland
As an Alien Nation's alienation
Transfixed to a cellphonic regeneration

In a neverget navigate node to node,
Hypnotically fleeing from bugs in a code,
From an evil gone viral through silicon trolls.
Poor droids, poor pod people, poor virtual souls,
                    Poor Caped Crusading heroes
                    Laocoön's sons in a world like Nero's.

Thence came the Nothing that Nobody saw,
In a rage of Reason and rule of war,
And the ratatatat of the technocrat
Stuns the thundering hoofbeats of Foss the Cat,
And the voice of the Scroobious Pipps
In light Pussybitten fyttes,
And the lays of the klupzian rubaiyat.
So crazed to the max with deep thoughts of payola
(Having drunk too much twenty-six ounce CocaCola)
None decided they know of a crazed ayatollah
Who's decided it's time to invade Pensacola
            Or maybe Peoria
            Would be much gorier
            Or that slattern Nogales or uptight Emporia.
All this is made clear, as they say you can see
In that first book of Samuel (chap. 15, verse 3).

So thoroughly armed with the crispy cream chrism
Of a piece with obeisant Deceptionalism,
            Like the kibbutzim turning outside in,
            Or a self-administered mickey finn
Or a Brook Farm transformed to a gated enclosure
In fear from indecent and public exposure,
What is it that's turned the jocose comatose?
It's the Nothing that Nobody knows.
What is it has laid out these byzantine plots
In quest for their deer-in-the-deadlight ersatz?
It's the love that has lefted them higher and drier
Like the justintime calls of the insider buyer.

And only loved Margo's loved lord called the Shadow
Knows the nothing that Nobody Knows,
Running in rivers of ruinous prose,
That prose
That grows
The Nothing that Nobody Knows.

Should Slobs Slur Brazil

"When you master a disaster in the Thaumaturgic Vale,
When the Streamen see the Seemen strive on bravely in a gale,
And the Katydadies leave their leafy lives decisively,
Will you won't you do you don't you don't you wonder (quietly)
Never how and whence the Twaddlequiver runs so musicly?"

"But we fear the Fraidies barking through a desolated Land,
Where the terrifying trippings of the Treemen hold command
While the Gleemen and the Gladyladies wander by the sea.
Do we dare we could we would we daren't wonder (piously)
(Never, Never!) where the Twaddlequiver runs so musicly?"

Then two faintly sadic Sadies in the Thaumaturgic Vale,
Drew two Dreamen into dreams of diabolics at a scale.
Fractured fractals mount a mountain to a grand deophony:
"Do you don't you do you don't you, don't you don't you don't you see?
Never more the river Twaddlequiver shall run phonicly."

"Never more? But hear now how that river's running phonicly.
Ever will the Twaddlequiver run on polyphonicly!"
"Never more the phonic river Twaddlequiver shall we see,
Never more, alas, the Twaddlequiver running out to sea."

Bedazed Went the Pollylops

From Dizzyland the Felssie folks
Afflicted with myopia
With Noduts and the Thoomsies threatened
Much loved Onomatopia
With vile Sputterbeanupps and Witches enspelled
On processed mac and cheese
While muscledup Stuperzero guards
Patrol in their SUVs.

They raised a mighty shout about
Onomatopic designs,
Led on by their Felssies day after day
And by night in their torchlit lines.

But as they came down like wolves on the fold
As if magic were turning what's wrong
In something from somewhere the Noduts first sensed
A disturbed and enveloping song.

"Has something wicked this way come?"
"Oh think not so, good Nodut!"
But just then out the Noduts slammed
As if a door had shut.

"How strange," the Felssies thought, "but still,
On, on" they drove the Thoomsies,
But with those words the Thooms dissolved
Like fadeouts in the movies.

"Think not our struggles nought avail!
Though some are fagged and falling,
We Felssies eye our selfsame prize, and
Judge those left, appalling.

"Oh be not troubled, do not fail
    These defections are just minor glitches
But like guttering candles that wink and die out
    Went the vile Sputterbeanups and Witches.

At these transhumanitions the Felssies were stumped,
    "It's as if they persist to desist.
My comrades keep fading, there's something pervading
    Like light in a luminous mist.

Oh you last of the valiant, stay true as blue glue
    To your deepsworn vows, Stooperzeroes !"
But like a war career or a bad idea,
    Brain-dead and gone went the heroes.

Then loud upon the winds arose
    The wails of all the Felssies.
"This life begins to taste, we think,
    Like mac and processed cheese.
Have mercy, Onomatopods,
    Forget what we've essayed here
Onomatopia, stay free!
    Forgive the raid we've made here."

The Felssies, Thoomsies, Stooperzeroes,
    Noduts and Sputterbeanupps
And Witches unbeknownst had got
    Poetics, intravenous —
And that is how was long since saved
    Onomatopia,
The modest Onomatopods,
    And music's cornucopia.

A Set for the Unsettled

The Wraith
(after William Blake)

Nosferatu, hear me,
Fateful angel, hear me
Light splits up nightstricken skies
Burning daylight through your eyes
Blissful tales of fear gone wrong
Sold to children for a song
Children of the night to feed
On the day's bewildered deeds
Little man god near me
Fateful angel hear me.

Nosferatu, listen,
Don't look now just listen
Forests hateful to the sun
Whisper what's been done undone
Tender feet you taught to tread
Ancient voices down and dread
To unlight the living dead
To benight the righteous dead
(Fast asleep and snug abed)
Mal d'aurore blesspheme us
Zbúrator unseem us.

Our Barbie

(after William Blake)

Barbie, Barbie, what a fright
All pinked out for death and blight
In the twinkling of your eye
You're the lady of Shanghai.

Why such pouting? Don't be cross.
Just forget Diana Ross.
Brush our teeth and fix our hair,
Don't forget to say your prayers.

So you fell into arrears
With those Women of Algiers?
Here all Hades' Módū ladies
Dream of driving your Mercedes.

Barbie, Barbie, that's a dear,
Toys away now, bedtime's here,
In the twinkie of your eye
We're on board now for Shanghai.

Girls

(after Joyce Kilmer)

We think that we would like to see
A god with all his history.

Like Somebody who feels hard pressed,
And knows his best is second best

A god made out of curds and whey
Or from that mess of potter's clay

Who might be best to disobey
Or — for our favor — lead astray

A god whose book's uncommon prayer
Discounts his tale of wear and tear

Who lives in an intense inane,
And falls real hard for Mary Jane.

(Oh say can you see, oh dear D. O. D.
Les belles dames sont damnées … ici.)

At Henry's Tomb
(after Henry Wadsworth Longfellow)

On the myth-minded slopes of Mount Yaanek,
        In a moment of madness of yore
While you slept, crept an overweight demon,
        Enspelled in perpetual war.

He came 'twixt the dark and the daylight,
        When the night was beginning to lower,
Tossing storms through our day's occupations,
        To befuddle our Children's Hour.

So a host on the slopes of Mount Yaanek,
        Like the fiends of Tsalal, once was mustered
Dreamed up by a Bishop of Bingen
        Who one morning had waked up quite flustered.

But athwart that fantastical whiteout
        And its vast blinding call, *tout de suite*
Ran a silence of still small voices
        And a scurry of resolute feet.

And all of that silence and soaring
        Was announcing beyond all surmise
That "your bishoprick days are extinguished
        In light shot from more numinous eyes."

Let me study to list to that music
        These muses from elsewhere prepare —
Old Nancy, Ayanna, and Lori,
        And Ilhan with jet black hair.

Their sudden rush from the stairway,
        Their sudden raid from the hall!

By three doors left unguarded
        They have breached my cherished wall!

Now they're climbing into my turret
        O'er the arms and back of my chair;
Though I tried to escape, they're around me;
        They seem to be everywhere.

So they overran my defenses
        And overtook all of my art,
And they shattered the hosts on Mount Yaanek
        And the Mouse Tower that once was my heart.

And they mean to set me forever
        In their secret moment each day
Till the walled up brawls of our ruin
        Fall like halls of sawdust away."

She dreams up creatures

(after Lord Byron)

I.

She dreams up creatures burning blight
    She casts amused indifferent eyes
Upon her children of the night,
    Her artistes trained to amortize
Games of beauty's flighty light
    Our gaudy everydays devize.

2.

Transhuman source and sorceress,
    How suddenly I meet your face's
Regimen to dispossess
    Intense inanities of grace.
Nightshade decor is your largesse
    You evanesce as you unlace.

3.

To you I make this deep sworn vow,
    You unheard sounds, reversed events,
Invent us here, preverb us now
    Disorient   perverse   dement
"A mind at peace with all below"
    Schooled to a stammer of assent.

Twas long ago they say it was
(after Scriptor Ignotus)

dies inlucescat et Lucifer oriature in cordibus vestris.
2 Peter 1: 19

‘Twas long ago, they say it was, that Jesus Christ arose,
But whether that in fact took place there’s nobody who knows.
        But maybe it’s important
        That each of us think through
If (by the rood!) there’s anything
In this old tale that’s true.

It is the case that in a poém Gertrude Stein once wrote,
“a rose ‘s a rose ‘s a rose ‘s a rose”, she outraged lots of folks,

Yet that’s both true and charming
Though promising no glory
It trans mutes what’s unpleasant in
That gory allegory.

If that’s not true, it’s charming
Though promising no glory
It slips past what confounds us in
That gory allegory.

I C U
(after Robert Frost)

Eating Up Poems of an Early Evening

“Whose words these are they only know
Who passage through the village Though.”
“Then why should I be stopping here?”
“I saw you stopping long ago.”

“Perhaps you’re just a puppeteer
And here we’re near the ghouls of Wier,
That would-be woodland. Is it fake?
I’m worried I might disappear.”

“What I misgive, you might mistake,
It’s all a game of give and take,
Heaving full or sliding neap.
I would the words ran wild awake.

Some words are promises asleep
And sleep brings promises that leak —
But whether maps are dark and deep
Our whether maps are dark and deep.”

*

Splendor in Grass on a Frostbit Evening

Perchance these woulds you wouldn’t know
Because they’re near the village though,
Though sin is taxed and cats career
Through tumbled weeds of Tampico.

Has splendor in that grass turned sere,
Has tea time fled this last frontier,

Was Mary Jane a bad mistake,
My mind's not right, should I stop here?

All night they're dreaming when they wake
Morning becomes a coffee cake.
That sere and yellow leaf? Good grief!
Mormons become the Great Salt Lake.

A good night's sleep's a real relief
For marmosets and disbelief.
And mice are nibbling at the sheep
The smiles of mice and miles of sheep.

Dearthbound in Heaven. (An Unfinished Synchrony)

(after Francis Thompson)

I led them every night and every day,
I fed them on their deadmarch through the years.
I then said– "well, if there's another way
Spill it, for Crissake". Then their hoots and jeers
Explode the buildings shake with demon laughter.
        Brutal and thoroughbred,
        On feral feet they fled,
Borne on their ancient seasonal careers,
    Indifferent to what comes before or after
        As rocks or trees or space
        As grace or as disgrace
    Betaking her or him or thee or me.
        No victory will defeat
    Their swaddled windingsheet
        Or fuck up their estranged affinity.

Kakis McGoonagil I, II
(after William Wordsworth)

I.

He felt his way along the way
A leading from above,
That tale to take your breath away —
A maid, a man, a dove,

Violence the *esprit de coeur*
Half hidden from the eye
Fear as a Missal's *aide-memoire*
And love a Long Goodbye.

He lived unknown, and few could say
When Kakis ceased to be
He passed along from grave to gay
Indifference to me.

II

Aslumber in the Great Irreal
(It lasted many years)
He felt he had no call to feel
The force of earthly fears.

"No motion has he now, no force,
He neither hears nor sees"
He hears no call to find recourse
In rocks and stones and trees.

Sissy's Fuss

(in two Miltonic fyttes)

Now nevermore that laureleiing lore
Of lovelorn turtles cooing ear to here
Undeafconned, nor those preludes Buxtehude
Left Bach himself unglued,
Looking for love in Lübeck past the drear
Heart's mountains in the downfall of that year,
And that juvescence we revere; nor you,
My sister sinister, nor Edward Lear
Nor inverse Edgar's, Ogden's, Stevie's climb
By mindflights through those vast Caucasians drear —
Oh, those naked mingled jingles, ah — who knew
Here was a weight to raise waylaying rhyme,
To plink and plunk upon a midnight queer
Heart mountings, happy flowers in a wind
Ye innocents and, yes, the goodly feere.

•

O lass! Does Puss in Boots dare this or care
At all, or Lochinvar's cute canon aid
Those dainty angels on their pleasure cruise?
The stately homes of England ? Why abuse
The hard of hearing with a hand grenade
Or parse a pony with a questionnaire?
Why ask? you ask. The point (to paraphrase
That You-Know-Who and much maligned
Magician of statistical malaise)
To prowl the conscious with unconscious Mind
Work out the long division of your days
By light-year measures, then enter Shakespeare's
Prose and measure it with Hemingway's
And split the difference, making "Two Cheers
For Democracy", one for Conan Doyle
(That's *Sir* Arthur Conan Doyle).
Now set off the odd remainder, downsize

The irrational, decimate edgewise
And track those unbecoming men that strove
With numbers (and the numbers came full speed).
So much for fame, so much for tumbleweed.

So Roll the Mad Dancers

(after the English of Lautréamont)

Frigment I

Let me call back the songs of those creatures, bare
and shining and sudden and momentarily imaginable
like the dreams he wants to dream, — let them remember the
lays of those angelic hosts and their
second and still-aborning radiance. And behold, their carrion come
for to fortify afire dies irae
set ablaze and longing toward extinction, their enchanted
eyes, for an instant turning to lips of jasper, foresee
a youth call out: Old Man, forget, forgive.

Frigment I, variant 1

Can it embellish the calm that the question, thought
and uttered of a sudden momentarily enviable
like what he is passing, may imagine in stanzas his
lines through the 14 or 15 pupils of these
fourth grade eyes and opportune exclamations? For unless he is able to
prove to his cacklings a noisy chicken and a cochinchina
fact equal at least to his propositions, the burlesque
droppings of this canting brute will score his hyperboles as
my mission insults his work.

Tang

A feint move in the cleft of the hills,
the hillwraith, her mantle hanging with moss,
ivy-girded eyes peer out. "Do you yearn
for me, who am so comely? I ride a red
leopard, striped lynxes attending, my flag
plaited cassia, my cloak stone-orchid, my sash
wild ginger, a gift for him I love. You can
find me here moving in this bamboo's darkness."
(lines worked from Ch'u Yuan's "Nine Songs")

•

You see best from the monastery of Chiang-yan,
blue houses of Yang-chou, the wineshops,
jade girls blowing tunes, "The gold frog gnaws at my lock"
"We are burning the noise of faint thunder"
and often
"Never let your heart open with spring flowers
One inch of love is an inch of ashes".

•

In a dream of heaven the rays slant white,
you peer down cassia-scented paths,
China! It's so far.

•

Call these words "the impersonator" —
you're better off writing than reading.
The sages wrote the books and the sages are dead.

•

He orders the city gates closed.

"So what of the banners! Here are tapestries,
And Love's listless bowmen,
Skilled needles, painless arrows."

Red everywhere, rushings, blue pennons on black poles,
"implacable hosts" overcoming overcoming.
And they sing coming on triumphantly
the studded gates gaping like stunned men,

"Didn't you hear anything!"
"They're closing. The distance. They're here,
They've been here, some of them, all along."

He ordered the city gates closed.
No one heard, the battle was over
long ago, now they sing in tapestries.
And they are here, distance closed,
the studded gates gape like stunned men.

•

The animals have discovered my poems,
they sit and learn them by letter by heart
in the wild called "Golden Bells" where gods
meet with loved friends.
Not here
on government pay the peony seasons, the seven-voiced
flowers go to market. So? Henceforth tied
to things beyond myself, taxed and transplanted, so?

•

Now the animals discover your poems,
sifting and learning by letter by heart
as wild gods call in "Golden Bells".

•

When a monkey's blow leaves you senseless
know that the demon's days are numbered.

•

Question.
Why need it be a dream, the poems
of the Virasaiva saints? Their metres are gods,
the arithmetic of strings and drums
their singing.
Answer.
There are so many gods
there's no place left
to put your feet.

•

The world tilts downward dreams
a vain recourse,
        searching for the shapes of letters

•

At "The definition of Impermanence" he said,
        Who imagines satisfied Pacifics, happy at their shores?"
"The sea grows old in it".

•

Moving you make no sound
raise no clouds of dust, your feet
touch the underhindered ground.
Nothing marks your presence or descent.

•

Her head bending near my shoulder — why
didn't I kiss her face. I am bent to be
ruined like a tree dragged down
swollen rivers, like a river
eroding its banks, uprooting trees,
roiled and stammering along.

•

Question.
Lost as you are in the Sonohara woodlands,
Why haste now to plunge in morning mists?

V
Four Last Poems

I had rather compose in a language almost dead
and for a people all but extinct.

Alfieri, *Memoirs*

Semele

There's nothing here on the page
that's important, blue distants
of the mind clear cutting across the cold white —
armed visions, black habits
behaving correctly
                                        we maintain
the property, the people
come here and stay here,
there's no place like home.

As there's nothing here the text begins
leaking like a weak bladder, so what
were you thinking to get beyond
the malfunctions of achievement
nothing will change,
                                        we will maintain
the property, the people
come here and stay here,
there's no place like home.

You there imagining yourself
doing what? These sentences eat
your words wearing thin like patients –
how do you measure the coast of England
or used gauze
                                        and still we maintain
the property, the people
come here and stay here,
there's no place like home.

HE. "The difficulties set you going and grow worse. Why stop to make repairs on the road of good intentions?"

SHE. “There is no good Will. Will is always evil. That’s what it’s for. Shipwrecking.”

HE. “I’ve spent too much time in libraries. Look at this prose, this life. It’s true. We unherit an archive needing constant attention. So you prepare yourself for the task, you study and are determined, deliberate. You learn to write by learning how badly you can do it. Again and again you pore over the records, this word, that form, where is it proper or best or even possible to say one thing or another. The dialects are endless, the words want your love and await your devotions, which you pay. In return they move along, and you arrive in the Sixth Chamber, a book among the books.” “Now you are the master of the archive. Do you also feel the parchment of your skin” – “When did that happen?” – “or if you’re puzzled can you make out the color of your blood?” “Is the question a game? Since everything seems clear, what exactly don’t I know?”

SHE. “Nothing is unknown. And nothing will change.”

HE. “Yes, the mutation of the texts. The texts discover their limits and play their endless games. From time to time they remember how to think through their bodies. And then new figures are born, historiated, ornamental. New pages from old rags, heavy now this warm young flesh, quick to the touch. Imagination enters, the sovereign of this place, the master printer. Bold types will kiss the pages and leave no marks behind.

“What stands beyond these alabaster rangers? An underworld
of broken codes, forbidding heavy water. You plunge
the impassibles, signals drone through radiated air. A question
gets repeated

what poem would break its heart to give back your life

what poem

would break its heart to give back your life

, a black cat

carries off the bodies of the living and the dead – sml3e, jjm2f,
passwords in the mirrors staring back, starving, living,
the heat-death of whitened black water. The room floods
with black crushed silk.”

SHE. "An underworld? Winds too living not on air but in these bodies you see
(I see), dragged along stone walls? And all the rest of it, my angel, all angels
of rain and lightening. Such tales. Suppose a fragile terra cotta figure fired
with fire. There I am unhollowed clay. My hand (you see) remembers something
in my sighs, that draped recess, if I could move I would be

bringing her fingers from lips to lips, she sucks them like a lollipop smiling like a child remembering a perfect day

Lines Found in the River Temple Near White Tiger Cave, by Chang Hsu

Long ago they fled the world, left human company.
sought the life of immortal spirits and never went back.
Wang Wei, "Source of the Peach Flower Stream"

You rule I realize the greatest city
and great men imagine entering
in triumph through the Gate of Jade
my queen,

never think I would ever think to come,
Peach Flower Stream moves the grass
along currents that have emptied my heart,
my pride,

your canopy of golden forests keeps
this dark retreated darkening so I see
rising like mists at Hanging Bridge, Red
Lotus Peak,

Flowered Pool, where no words can sing or think
what is there to say, grassy stream and perpetual,
Two Fishes Side by Side, clinging to a branch
Dark Cicada,

Turning Dragons float through bamboo
near the altar, butterflies of the Flying Hand
spin cocoons beside a dwarfed pine,
Singing Monkey,

soft knives at your fingertips lopping
birds of paradise reeling, scattering
along the eight valleys running
Little Stream,

sing in the second style of golden
gullies, sing again Water-Chestnut Teeth
deeper through the valley's chambers rising

Lute Strings

strung in the trees, the jays screaming,
messengers from the blue unfound of blue,
breathing waters, and at the end, towers

my underworld,

this poem being written to a queen,
a scholar of Su Nu arrives at one,
one being the queen's hour and one to find

her aspiration.

A Commentary on the Lost "River Temple" Lines by Chang Hsu

The epigraph from Wang Wei demonstrates that this text of the poem has been copied or perhaps reconstituted after the lost original: for the lines from Wang Wei come from a well-known poem written in response to Chang Hsu's famous verses.

This reconstituted style, if one may so call it, signals the artfulness of the work: specifically, the presence of the principal theme of the necessity of art. The person responsible for this "sweet new style" remains, like the queen addressed in the poem, unnamed and unknown. Anonymity becomes then a second-order fact in the work, signaling another important theme: immediated art as the locus of absolute and even transubstantial values.

We should pause here before turning to the third and final great theme being pursued in the poem. The necessity of immediated art. The double theme enters at once in the first strophe and (as one expects) returns more explicitly in the last. "The greatest city" is the queen herself. It is also the city of the scholar and the artist, and the city aspired to by the poet and all poets, the "great men" who have imagined "entering" its precincts. But Chang Hsu's art will not imagine the possibility of such a triumph. He undertakes no adventures, no wars, he stays far from the Imperial City, near the temple of the Peach Flower Stream, whose flowing waters symbolize the life to which he aspires ("her aspiration").

But all the poem's personal and political figurations – all of its immediate references – are cast into artful literary allusions. These preserve the poem's deepest transubstantial commitments, its order of reality

(Wang Wei's "life of immortal spirits") toward which the text's symbolic forms keep pointing.

The most important of these forms of art will not be found among the images, those arresting (and artfully distracting) visibilities. It emerges recurrently and obliquely as the poem's undergrounded syntax that drives the verbs of continuing presence and action.

So it is that "this poem is being written" and that the poet makes no move beyond his river temple retreat.

So it is that the first two themes run and converge "along currents that have emptied my heart/ my pride". The poet discovers and defines his own discipline in the acts that empty him out, and that expose the failure by which he alone will measure his success.

So it is that he remains a "scholar" to the end, like the Han emperor Huang Ti, who took instruction in the Arts of Love from Su Nu, as the ancient dialogues tell.

That artful indirection reveals what the text has been holding in suspension: the full revelation of the poem's third great theme. Though a continuous if secret presence from the first, it has been held "in reserve" to perpetuate imaginative intensity.

It is the theme of the identity of Love and Poetry and the artifices that enable both. The "one to find" is at once the queen, the poet, and their union; the act of poetry, the act of love, and their identity; the time of these acts, "the life of immortal spirits", and their connection along the currents of Peach Flower Stream.

Line Notes.

Strophe 1, line 3. Gate of Jade, the principal gate of the queen's city. The poet is playing with a Tao figure for the vulva. That figure is a special focus of attention in the dialogues and treatises on the Art of Love written in the dynasties before the Tang, where it becomes a complex convention. The subsequent strophes make a rich display of Taoist figures.

Strophe 2, line 2. Peach Flower Stream is the focus of the Chang Hsu poem that called out Wang Wei's response. The grass is a coded reference to Chang Hsu, whose calligraphy (grass writing) was judged one of the three wonders of the Age (see also strophe 4, line 2).

Strophe 3, line 3. "Hanging Bridge" is another reference to Chang Hsu's poem. It is a figural reference to the key Taoist discipline of "coitus reservatus", which is itself a transubstantial figure drawing on the commitment to poetry as an artful practice.

Strophe 6, line 1. A bold image, the only original figure in the poem. At the text's second order it calls to the poem's key ideas, artifice and reserve. It's aesthetic/erotic significance bridges the valley that the poem enters and explores and within which its textual stream runs.

Why I am not a Poet, II

1. The Shewing

I shall wholly break you of your vain affections and your vicious pride; and after that I shall gather you together and make you mild and meek, clean and holy, by oneing to me.

(Julian of Norwich, *Revelations of Divine Love*)

Do they see you as a book? Each breathtaking gold miniature of flesh
and form turning eternal? Ornamental flames burn beneath your feet, ravishing the Light,
my Lady,
and tempests of lechery break across these fair abstractions.
Who will write the metamorphoses of escape, the wars to make belief?
And these words I don't quite disbelieve? The poems
I tried to make them say "not yet, don't go". Then each word snaps its switch: this is dark, this, this, this
All of this is dark. Faithless
I am slowly emptied from the mouth of my words.

Also I heard a bodily jangling, as if it had been of two persons, and both,
to my thinking, jangled at one time as if they had holden a parliament with
a great busy-ness, and all was soft muttering, so that I understood nought
that they said. And all this was to stir me to despair.

I was sleeping through the corridors of prose, in dreams of aversion,
"We are aversive to the absolute
We will not serve, they say."
Did cold winds bring you then – six, five, three years ago? – turning my head to imagine what I couldn't imagine? Then I saw your face wearing the mask of my imaginations. The last word was your face wearing a mask of my illusions.

I saw His sweet face as it were dry and bloodless with pale dying. And
later, more pale, dead, languoring; and then turned more dead unto blue;

and then more brown-blue, as the flesh turned more deeply dead. For His Passion shewed to me most specially in His blessed face (and chiefly in His lips): there I saw these four colours, though it were afore fresh, ruddy, and pleasing, to my sight. This was a pitiful change to see, this deep dying. And also the inward moisture clotted and dried, to my sight, and the sweet body was brown and black, all turned out of fair, life-like colour of itself, unto dry dying. Bloodlessness and pain dried within; and blowing of wind and cold coming from without met together in the sweet body.

I thirst.

Out of the last crucial stations of that fiction
splinters of black
because there are still things   I sometimes think   I want to see
my disbelief is not quite perfect
and this is what "never truly being" means to be
"devinir immortel et puis morire"
"like a candle blown out
at the limit of its flame"   and still to be
not yet quite   disbelieving still   there is

the transubstantial world
we have assumed   its inner standing point   and its argument
proceeding through a seizure of absence.
"I saw God in a point." "I am the Ground."
What ground? Who sees anything?
The logic of love, is it true, will we disappear like false conclusions?

And anon I was sore ashamed and astonished for my recklessness, and I thought: This man taketh in sober earnest the least word that I might say. Then said I no more thereof. And when I saw that he took it earnestly and with so great reverence, I wept, full greatly ashamed, and would have been shriven.

There are forms moved by discretion, like snakes, ring by gathering ring. They are splendid, camouflaged, abandoned, they evacuate the air.

Incensed with memories, the call comes for a language that behaves, a tongue that answers hovers listens thinking. Or moves to your body like a pair of dancing hands. The skills we want to know we have to learn again that day each day, that day when nothing will be left to imagination. Blinded eyes flood with light, stand at fierce attention.

now in this life by many privy touchings of sweet spiritual sights and feeling, measured to us as our simpleness may bear it. And this is wrought, and shall be, by the grace of the Holy Ghost, so long till we shall die in longing, for love

2. L (fleur de Lis)

I'll never write your shape   again it's clear.

("Refraction Journal")

"A distinction can be made." And is, as L. From that shape I once, before I knew you, saw emerge the Laws of Form. That fleshless population of particulars, signs and their characters, all that once was here, do you remember? Laid to waste. Sold off for a song.

"A fig for those by Law protected!
    Liberty's a glorious feast!
Courts for cowards were erected
    Churches built to please the Priest."

L means the city is abandoned   loved, left, lost. There are, the poets think, always other cities left to burn. And this city? Burn it up, it is weighed in the balance and found wanting. Never again that surplus of surplus values, living in the myth of always being here, telling us what we're not.

"Life is all a Variorum
    We regard not how it goes,
Let them cant about decorum
    Who have character to lose."

Are you laughing goddess, as I come again my second coming sees the ruin at your fingernails. “The world will little note nor long remember what we say here, but it can never forget what they did here.” There is a resurrection, you insist. A maimed tooth announces a torment when your happiness forgets to care. And then I come again into a copse of faint scripts that once I stumbled on when I got lost as usual in your eyes. You see me, don’t you, returning there each day in secret and insane, like a widowed man to the grave of his love.

So I disremember you into random parts, that day I want to murder to dissect all that I’ve accomplished. This is the scattering of every trance of what we have imagined to be substantiation.

Poems as frail as threadbare cloths of love – the sick, the ecstatic, the judgmental. Their lovers will be faithless, the most that we can hope for. Why imagine something else? Some other language, some other set of devotions?

I have no idea how you move your hands.

3. The Telling

The author of a universal letter is a story-teller rather than an actor or a dancer.... . Its author is telling the story to himself as if it were all the stories and he the personified fascination of all imaginable listeners.
Laura Riding, *Everybody's Letters*

angel,   far angelica,   Madonna
beings beyond
the apparent heavens of their images we see
words that aren't being said, acts
of immediate entirety, "not as it were
from her mouth or in his eyes, but distinctly
between them", like threads of gold
Ligatured in this little room the faithful
forms drawn in simply as a breath

imperative messages are being
exchanged
color coded for the foreign faithless
ever fluent vocables: "Remain vexed with emptiness,

last poem,

um in Zauberkreis der Nacht
tief und tausendfach zu leben,

make yourself a study of inert precisions, think
in stone awareness of an unbreathed air

turning your worded mind through things untoward
each absolute impersoned name, desire to be

"consumed within a music of consuming". A serpent's tongue
tattooes the liquifying souls

carved crystal second comings,
"A something overtakes the mind"

the archived white mirages of arrival, Dis
ordering the senses, the encrypted city's

buildings of Los and arising, black being
with your skin of brain and transfixed rust:

come to no life unless you are
ready to die utterly to let life take over

around us sea
the aisles of grease
quell giorno piu non vi
leggemmo avanti
                                    that day no longer we
                                                                        read on

“Though Inland Far We Be”

ch’a l’abito de l’arte ha man che trema

Dante, *Paradiso*

The Scholar's Art

(for David Greetham)

certain cultures will not yield to force
care won't do nor will not even virtue
one needs patience hunting up a source

to go a journey start without previsions
feed off a land that people have been feeding
expect nothing when you make decisions

rites of passage call you to attention
gods exist to watch and to demand
disgrace awaits to undermine convention
grace to come to underwrite invention

"Though Inland Far We Be"

De omni re scibili [et quibusdam aliis]

"I'm not good imagining
a place that got to know
how being is belonging.
In winter there's snow

and cold no New Yorker ever
dreamed escaping from.
What's to imagine there where
animals would call it home

if they could talk like you?
This Third Coast – a digression
sometimes jerks me back to
it. In the West the sun

is king. Back East they fret
too much. This is different,
this middling bit
of Michigan. It doesn't

change too much I think
it's more substantial like a face
a porch, a hand, a drink
of water with a taste

of sulfur, houses built
on sand and then something
that looks to leave one lost
out here for words."

"Nothing

takes much to tilt a whirl.
Why don't you
stop by? We'll sit a while
outside, we two like two

for tea and talk about spring's
odd arrivings or the fall,
or summer peaches, berrying
near the lake, – and what all

else besides. Call again
any time, the thing
is nothing's to imagine,
there'll be just us talking."

Afterword

JANET KAUFFMAN

Approaching Jerome McGann's *Transubstantiations* from a Wetland (or other Ecosystem)

Transubstantiation is an immense word. Invisible and instantaneous, it is powerful in whatever realm claims it — ecclesiastic, alchemic, or mythical. Or poetical. It crosses boundaries, and shifts instantaneously this to that. Jerome McGann's book of poems, *Transubstantiations*, is a multitudinous, sometimes hilarious, game-playing, tormented, and deeply provocative collection from decades of his writing. It is the plural of his title, the multiple transubstantiations, that link many of the poems, rattle their territories, and provide both the weight and the lift to this book.

I met Jerry McGann more than 50 years ago in graduate school at the University of Chicago. We've kept in touch over years, through generations. The fullness of his life as a textual scholar encompasses at least three centuries of past poetries, up to and including digital archival projects. He has lived with many of the archives we "unherit.... Again and again, you pore over records, this word, that form, where is it proper or best or even possible to say one thing or another." (from "Semele," in the section "Four Last Poems").

That's always the question. Even here. I'll try to say one thing or another.

In many of these poems, McGann balances or reverses or flips what you might call transubstantial equations, not so much Take this bread/it is my Body, or wine = blood, but other transubstantials: sense/nonsense; not this/not that; Neti, Neti; this/this; poet/not a poet; Poetry/Love; mortality/immortality, and variants, "to become immortal then to die."

My framework for almost all things is ecological, not scholarly. So before reading too far, I carried *Transubstantiations* on a walk to the wetland. No particular reason. Just a body carrying *Transubstantiations* to the wetland. But once there, I did open the pages, touched the paper, looked at the empty spaces, the pattern of lettering. I thought I smelled ink. Is it still vegetal ink these days? I read a few lines, voiced them. Listened. And noticed, a waver — from my lungs to grasses, the words were moving air. The words were air.

…There are forms moved by discretion, like snakes, ring by gathering ring. They
are
splendid, camouflaged, abandoned, they evacuate the air.
Incensed with memories, the call comes for a language that behaves, a tongue
that answers hovers listens thinking….
from "Why I am not a Poet II"

And, out loud, moving even more air, tympanic, words from "Aenigma: An Image (in a Game)", these lines from section "M
emory"—

… Mobile numbers, summon somewhere
music, numbing sermons. Magellan's whimsical
embracing magic — amorous Moroccan
zombies stumble, impale themselves;
immense motors, miserere nobis — impinge, impel…

McGann's poems are not only compelling as visual texts, the lettering and conglomerate shapes of words, line arrangements, they are also deeply textural, layered and contoured, forms metamorphosed— his literary sources are wide-flung, and free-wheeling, and language sources are ancient, back to first syllables. His poetry mines all those veins, an unmatched richness. And while I've seen many of his poems over the years, this collection's first poem, "The Cryptography of Edgar Poe," and the mid-section, titled like the book, "Transubstantiations", were new to me. As was the phenomenal section, "Last Four Poems" — more on that in a bit.

"The Cryptography of Edgar Poe" is set apart at the beginning, the title a prelude to the play with language and forms to come. The poem is a "transubstantiation" of Mallarmé's "The Tomb of Edgar Poe" — a transmogrified! translation. McGann twists and improvises from the start. A phrase like "fouled contaminate concoction" didn't have that kick in earlier English translations, where a "black mire" was the more likely wording. And most telling of the free-style hand of McGann is "the *gorious* tomb of Poe" (my italics). No "gilded" or "golden" or "dazzling," no 19th C. "glorious."

McGann introduces his language-at-large, at play or in torment, a perpetual reconsideration — graffitied honorifics from now.

Jumping for a moment to the mid-section collection, its title now plural, Transubstantiations, is comprised of two sections: "A Set for Edward Lear and Lewis Carroll" and "A Set for the Unsettled." These poems are a dizzying core to McGann's book, with parodic and expert juggling of structures, styles, even Blake's, one of the Unsettled ones — the nonsense and mimicry a heartfelt nod to the range and forms of poetry McGann knows by heart, and to Sense transubstantiated to not-a-Poet's Nonsense.

From the Lear and Carroll set — from "The Nothing That Nobody Knows"

> . . .
> Thus an awful darkness and silence arose
>   Across that besimulate land,
> Like a cheese soufflé or that bubbly prose —
>   "Like when," "Like say" — like, bland
> As an Alien Nation's alienation
> Transfixed to a cellphonic regeneration
> In a neverget navigate node to node,
> Hypnotically fleeing from bugs in a code . . .

Or, from the Unsettled group — from "Girls (after Joyce Kilmer)"

> We think that we would like to see
> A god with all his history.
>
> Like Somebody who feels hard pressed,
> and knows his best is second best
>
> A god made out of curds and whey
> Or from that mess of potter's clay.
>
> Who might be best to disobey
> Or — for our favor — lead astray…

It's a wild ride, that middle section, a core exercised.

Wherever his language lands, McGann cannot and does not deny he's a Scholar of poetry. Whereas — in not one but two poems in the book — he does deny he's a Poet: "Why I am not a Poet I" and "Why I am not a Poet II." And elsewhere McGann describes himself in the third-person, in this brief prefatory note: "…Like his namesake, he is devoted to scholars and scholarship. He has sometimes written verse, which he is certain always in the end aspires to the condition of Nonsense, which it sometimes achieves." Yes indeed. We are witnesses to it.

Surrounding, embracing these central sense-with-nonsense poems are the poems spanning McGann's lifetime as researcher, scholar, human being. For many of us not scholars, reading his poetry becomes partly a physical activity — the bits of Italian, German, Sanskrit, names and unfamiliar phrases often had me moving, from the page to Translate apps online, to his previous books, to Wikipedia summaries and beyond, far beyond! — most wonderfully discovering treasures like Julian of Norwich and her *Revelations of Divine Love.* How could I not have heard of her ever? The digressive searches and arrows off course are a quest map to remote wandering and expansive discoveries in McGann's poetry.

Such as, at one point, puzzling: I looked up, then back to the page. I'd just read a second occurrence of the phrase "skin of brain," in "last poem,". It's a phrase in the title of an early poem,"Being with a Skin of Brain," where its association is with tremendous loss, of touch, of the mind, whatever had been, in dire torment, as first the eyes in the poem, then eventually "…the body/turns dust and water to a crystal suit of nerves./ No hand will touch/ what once was flesh, the mind sets hard/ acrylic… lucid black/thoughts grow/their final skin of brain, the steel electric/field of forms…"

McGann is not deterred by dark. And when "skin of brain" recurs in "last poem," the language carries even more darkness and finality, there's now "… with your skin of brain and transfixed rust:/come to no life unless you are/ ready to die utterly to let life take over…." Certain phrases and life/death, mortal/immortal transubstantials thread throughout McGann's poetry.

Most noticeably, there's the broad attention to the ultimate, often impossible, choices — dying "to let life take over," as in that "last poem," or its recurrent alternative, 'To become immortal, then to die,' a line from Godard's *Breathless*, which first appears in McGann's early poem "Dead End." That poem offers a wide cinematic scope: "…If God laid out the world on an anvil/and the blows beat out like Blake, infinity/would rush up howling in your face/…Noise at that superlative becomes a place /where you could see far at the end a door/if you were to go on would you open it/if you knew you would understand at last/'simply everything'? That is where ambition stops:/'To become immortal, then to die'…."

And again, in "Why I am not a Poet II," in darker and more specific terms, this same transubstantial, "be immortal/then to die" appears. This poem is an extraordinary, extended back and forth, call-and-response, a difficult almost-dialogue, with Julian of Norwich's *Revelations of Divine Love*, her 14th Century account of visitations from various forms of the Divine in her sickroom. After one such vision, she details Jesus's "deep dying." How his "…Bloodlessness and pain dried within; and blowing of wind and cold coming from without met together in the sweet body…"

The response, in part:

…there are still things   I sometimes think   I want to see
my disbelief is not quite perfect
        and this is what it means "never truly being" means to be
"devinir immortel et puis morire"
"like a candle blown out
at the limit of its flame" and still to be
not yet quite   disbelieving still   there is

the transubstantial world
we have assumed   its *inner standing point*   and its argument
proceeding through a *seizure of absence.*
"I saw God in a point." "I am the Ground."
What ground? Who sees anything?…   [my italics]

This language, struggling to locate the transubstantial, an idea so impossible and inexplicable in language, we most likely, most of us, picture a kind of cartoon swap, bread to body, wine to blood, mortality/immortality, whichever way the transubstantials are presented, flicking on/off.

But the insufficiencies of language infuse McGann's poetry, intensify it, especially in these overwhelming "Four Last Poems", their territories of belief, love, language, poetry. The destabilizing phrases I italicized above, for instance: "not yet quite," "inner standing point," "seizure of absence"

— they somehow shimmer. While language as open as that, and indefinite, refuses to clarify, the phrases nonetheless harbor potential spaces for language to shift, transubstantiate, reveal.

These generative holding spaces in McGann's language are for me the way the "Four Last Poems" conceive a transubstantiated Poetry. In another of the "Four Last Poems", "Lines Found in the River Temple Near White Tiger Cave by Chang Hsu," the Commentary section notes a similarly hidden but generative path of emergence:

> "…the poem's deepest transubstantial commitments … will not be found among the Images, those arresting (and artfully distracting) visibilities. It emerges recurrently and obliquely as the poem's undergrounded syntax that drives the verbs of continuing presence and action."

Transubstantial mychorrhizals of poetry! An "undergrounded" syntax. Verbs of continuing presence. What I love about McGann's depth of reading and scope of thought is the serious play of it, the hard drives and soft landings. The torment, the reprieves.

In "Lines Found …," with its complicated layers of materials and murky sources (Wang Wei's epigraph purportedly drawn from an unnamed poem that noted the original "Lines…" may have been "copied or perhaps reconstituted after the lost original," this according to the unspecified Commentary writer/scholar), we've got a multi-layered, "immediated art."

The "shimmering" I see in some phrases may be a twitch in my eye. But no matter how many overlapping layers of lostness or fabrication are involved, the revelations, transubstantiations, or "themes," as the Commentator notes, move nonetheless on through that "undergrounded syntax" to verbs of "continuing presence," and at last reach the "great" theme, "the identity of Love and Poetry…. the act of poetry, the act of love, and their identity;* …"

* albeit, full disclosure, the line concludes — "…the time of these acts, 'the life of immortal spirits,' and their connection along the currents of Peach Flower Stream." Which could hold things off a while.

However remote, unclaimed, or suspect the sources, we do not doubt this transubstantiation, the Identity of Love and Poetry, having read it (and seen it confirmed as to timing in the poem!). We believe — since it does appear that transubstantiation occurs (always? only?) in language, its poetry. There is also no doubt one transubstantial begets another. In McGann's poetry they are continuing presences. We know them when we see them.

From what may be an "inner standing point," look out, don't miss these lines in McGann's "last poem," — the grievous and passionate, nonsense and sense of the transubstantial world.

> "… come to no life unless you are
> ready to die utterly to let life take over
>
> around us sea
> the aisles of grease…"

About the Author

While poetry has been the focus of Jerome McGann's work throughout his long career as a scholar of language and culture, his own poetry, which he has been writing for more than 50 years, is not widely known. That's because, as he has often said, "I am not a poet." Most of the pieces here were privately printed, though some were published (often anonymously) in periodicals. "I couldn't see how to 'be a poet' in my place and time, and I've always been amazed by those who found the means to do it. For me, using this ancient form of expression has been a way of studying the fortunes and misfortunes of poetry and verse – and perforce of human language and society – by practicing some of their routines. I have felt the increasing urgency of this work as language and culture have been in our lifetimes translated into the data and information forecast by philosophies of engineering."

So this very literary book has a very unliterary "feel". Emily Dickinson might have called it "a kangaroo among the beauties" – something like McGann's Edgar Poe: "a god-forgotten darkling starling, non-indigenous American and, as such, sometimes disagreeable."

The book will appear shortly before McGann's last major project: his fully restored edition of Jaime de Angulo's great Ovidian salute to the languages and cultures of Native California, *Old Time Stories* (University of Chicago Press).